LEARNING GAMES WITHOUT LOSERS

By Sarah Liu and Mary Lou Vittitow

Incentive Publications, Inc.
Nashville, Tennessee

ISBN 0-86530-039-9

ABOUT THE BOOK . . .

In developing these activities for our own classrooms, it was our goal to make learning more fun and to meet the needs of students with differing backgrounds and abilities. We found them very helpful and hope that you do, too.

The games are designed to be compact and portable so that they do not require a lot of space in the classroom. Many can be used individually, which removes the threat of competition for the less capable student. The games may be used to strengthen skills in a deficient area and to allow the student to work without peer pressure or fear of failure. At the other end of the spectrum, the more gifted student may move through the activities much more quickly and participate in the more competitive games, thus avoiding the boredom that often plagues the very capable child.

We illustrated each game in order to help the teacher in making the game; however, do not feel bound to use the same words, facts or dialogue shown. We have often used the same game with several different skill levels and even in different content areas. For example, the same game can be used for the simplest addition facts or for division by two-digit numbers. These games are merely intended to be tools for teaching. The skill needed and level of difficulty may be tailored by each teacher to meet the needs of the class.

We have also included reproducible activity sheets varying in subject matter and level of difficulty.

We wish to dedicate this book to Chet Vittitow in appreciation for his help.

Sarah Liu
Mary Lou Vittitow

HELPFUL HINTS

Listed below are a few ideas that have proved helpful to us:

1. It is helpful to the children if parts of the game are kept together with the game board. Zippered plastic bags serve this purpose well. These can be attached to the games with notebook rings. Eyelet punchers sold in sewing and notion departments make sturdy holes in the game boards and bags.

2. Games need to be attractive (use lots of contrasting colors) as well as durable. We suggest laminating all the games and their parts. However, if laminating film is not available, clear contact paper makes a good substitute.

3. After a game is laminated, only permanent felt tip pens will write on it. Two brands we have had success with are:

   Broad tip: El Marko permanent marker by Flair
   Thin point: Sanford's Sharpie

4. Games that are made attractively should be displayed where they catch the attention of the children. We suggest game racks similar to the display shelves found in card shops or grocery stores, etc.

5. Do not let a lack of artistic ability discourage you from trying these activities. We have found parents to be a rich resource. They are often very capable and willing to copy and assemble games.

6. Old game boards can often be adapted for many of these games. The children are usually very happy to bring some from home.

7. We have found it helpful to have several copies of many of these games because often a group of children is working simultaneously on the same skill.

TABLE OF CONTENTS

ROBOT PEEK-THROUGH

SUBJECT AREA: Language Arts

SKILL: Dividing and accenting syllables

ADAPTABILITY: Question and answer type activities

MATERIALS: Tagboard, X-acto knife, felt pens

CONSTRUCTION:

Step 1: Cut tagboard into a robot shape (as in illustration).

Step 2: Cut out rectangles big enough for the words that will be used.

Step 3: Write the words on the front of the robot, below the rectangles.

Step 4: Write the correct syllabic division and accents on the back of the board, below the rectangles.

PLAYING DIRECTIONS: The student places a piece of paper under the robot and writes through the cut-out rectangles the correct division of syllables and accents for the words under each rectangle. Answers can be checked by flipping the robot over and placing it on top of the paper.

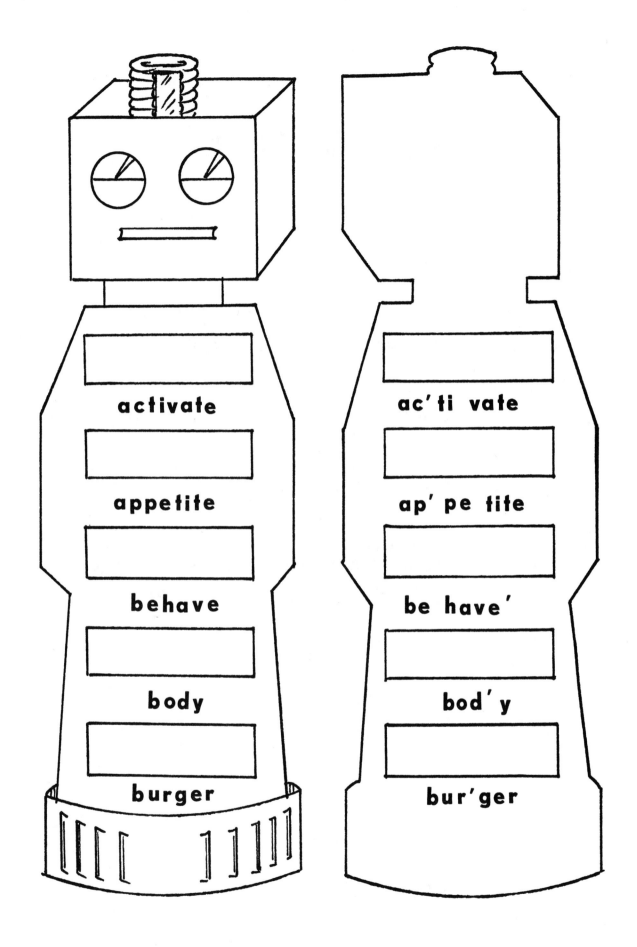

activate

appetite

behave

body

burger

ac′ti vate

ap′ pe tite

be have′

bod′y

bur′ger

SYNONYM STACK-UP

SUBJECT AREA: Language Arts

SKILL: Synonyms

ADAPTABILITY: Math facts, homonyms, antonyms, parts of speech

MATERIALS: Tagboard, felt pens, ruler, scissors, glue

CONSTRUCTION:
    Step 1:   Draw a pyramid on the tagboard similar to the illustration shown.
    Step 2:   Write the synonyms on the triangles.
    Step 3:   Cut the triangles apart.

PLAYING
DIRECTIONS: The student matches the synonyms. If all the synonyms are matched correctly, the pieces will form a pyramid.

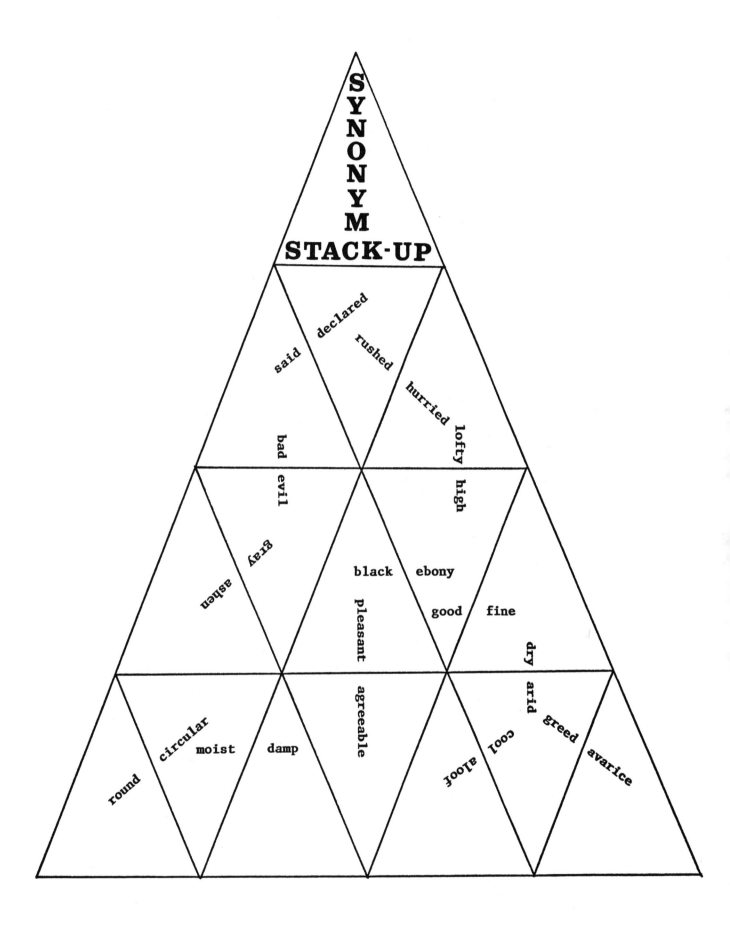

SYNONYM STACK-UP

said declared
rushed hurried lofty
bad evil high
gray ashen black ebony
pleasant good fine
round circular moist damp agreeable dry arid greed
cool aloof avarice

CONSONANT CHOO-CHOO

SUBJECT AREA: Language Arts

SKILL: Beginning consonants

ADAPTABILITY: Math combinations, number recognition, color recognition

MATERIALS: Posterboard, felt pens, construction paper, Mystik tape, magazines, scissors, tagboard, glue

CONSTRUCTION:

Step 1: Cut posterboard to 28" x 20".

Step 2: Cut twenty 4" x 3¾" pieces of different colored construction paper for cars.

Step 3: Fold each piece to make an envelope.

Step 4: Cut out a black engine, red caboose and forty-two wheels.

Step 5: Glue the engine, train cars, caboose and wheels to the posterboard.

Step 6: Write consonants on the train cars.

Step 7: Cut twenty-one 2½" x 2" cards from tagboard.

Step 8: Glue magazine pictures close to the top of the cards.

PLAYING DIRECTIONS: The student matches each picture card to the correct beginning consonant train card.

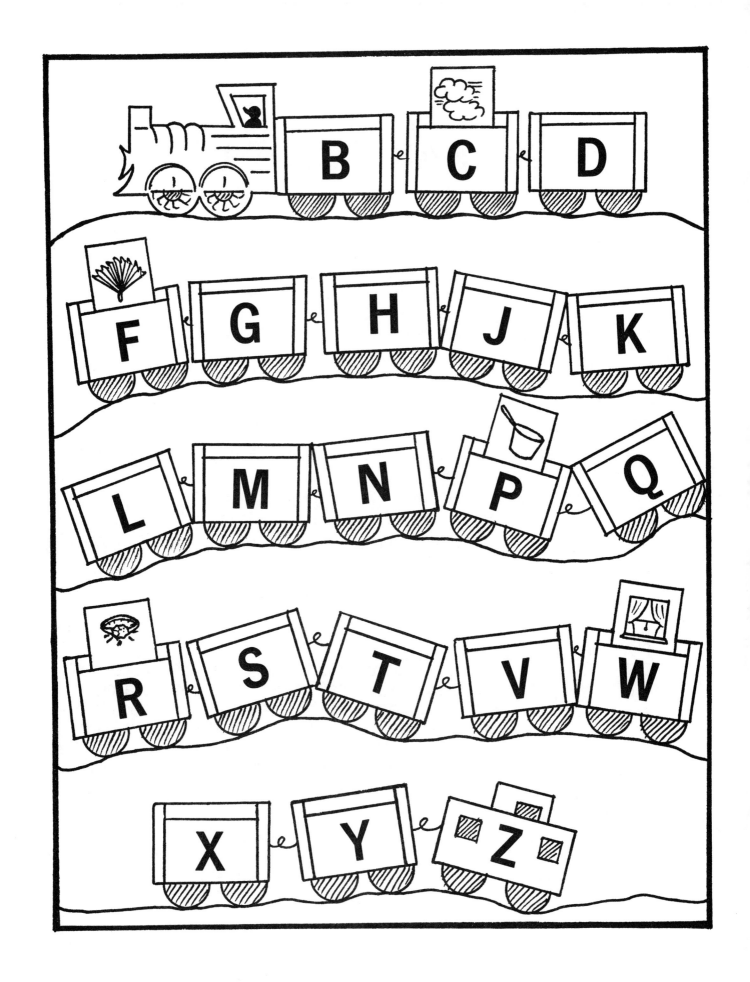

ALPHABET LINE-UP

SUBJECT AREA: Language Arts

SKILL: Alphabetizing

ADAPTABILITY: Number sequence

MATERIALS: Tagboard, X-acto knife, ruler, scissors, felt pens,
3" x 5" index cards

CONSTRUCTION:

    Step 1:   Cut four pieces of tagboard 5" x 12" to serve as card holders.

    Step 2:   Starting 1½" from the top, cut ten slits measuring 3½" across, leaving 1" spaces between the slits.

    Step 3:   Cut tagboard cards 2½" x 3" (or cut 3" x 5" index cards in half).

    Step 4:   Write the words on the cards that are to be alphabetized.

PLAYING DIRECTIONS: Two, three or four students may play this game. Deal out five cards and one card holder to each player. As each card is dealt, the players immediately place it in alternate slits, starting with the top slit. Each player takes a turn, moving only one card with each turn. The goal is to have the cards in alphabetical order with the least number of moves. The player who puts the cards in alphabetical order first wins.

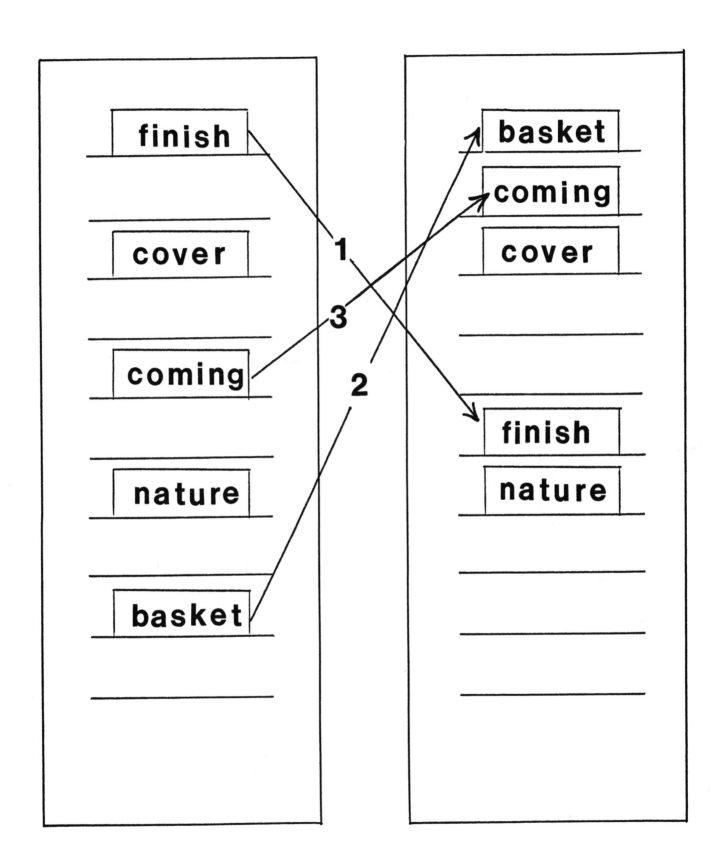

SPIN-A-VOWEL

SUBJECT AREA: Language Arts

SKILL: Vowels

MATERIALS: Posterboard, spinner, felt pens, scissors

CONSTRUCTION:

Step 1:   Cut a posterboard circle approximately 4" in diameter.

Step 2:   Divide the circle into five sections and write a vowel on each section.

Step 3:   Make two cards, 5½" x 4½".

Step 4:   Write three, four, or five-letter words on the cards, omitting the vowels. For example: b ___ t, sp ___ nd, h ___ t, d ___ ck, ch ___ ck, dr ___ p, sl ___ sh.

Step 5:   Attach a suction spinner to the circle. If not available, insert a brad in the center of the posterboard circle, and then place a paper clip so that it serves as a spinner.

PLAYING DIRECTIONS: Two students can play. The first player spins and attempts to use that vowel in one of the words on the card. If the vowel cannot be used in a word that makes sense, the player loses a turn. The next player then spins. The player who fills the card first wins.

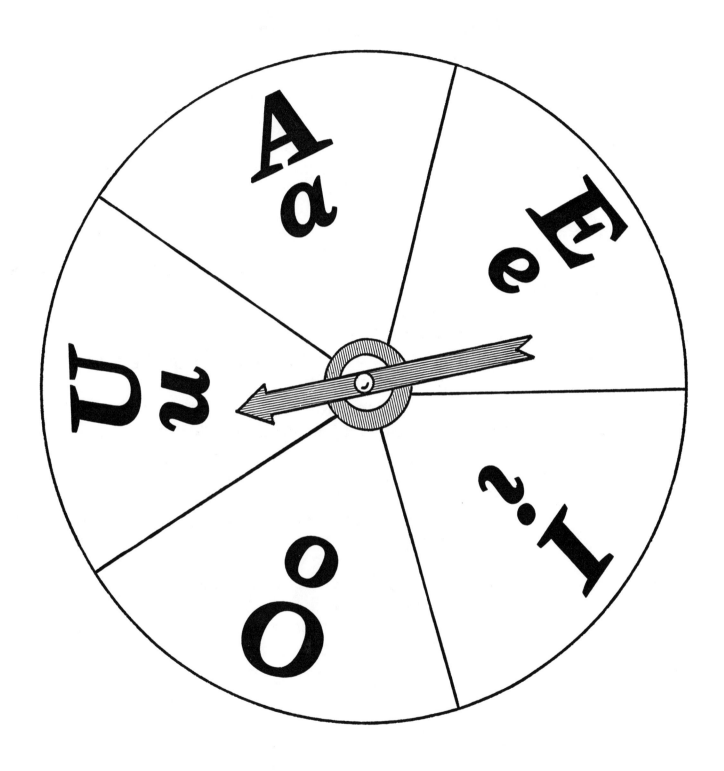

SPACE FANTASY

SUBJECT AREA: Language Arts

SKILL: Creative writing

MATERIALS: Posterboard, brads, decals or pictures, felt pens, ruler, scissors

CONSTRUCTION:

Step 1:   Cut a piece of posterboard measuring 12½" x 9" and decorate it with decals or pictures.

Step 2:   Cut a window 6¼" x 1", placing it 3" from the outer edges and 4" from the top of the board.

Step 3:   Cut two circles approximately 3½" in diameter and divide each circle into eight equal segments.

Step 4:   On one circle, write names of characters such as: astronaut, robot, Martian, moon god, slimy creature, Saturn warrior, Jupiter princess, Neptune ghost.

Step 5:   On the other circle, include activities such as: invaded the earth, ate rocks, had the power of magic, conquered space, fell in love with a spaceship, lost the battle, kidnapped the children of human beings, came to visit me, did away with evil.

Step 6:   Attach the circles with brads 2" from the outer edge and 4½" from the top.

PLAYING DIRECTIONS: The student spins the circles to determine the subject for creative writing.

SPACE FANTASY

A Martian

who fell in
love with a
spaceship

POCKETFUL OF RIDDLES

SUBJECT AREA: Language Arts

SKILL: Digraphs

ADAPTABILITY: Consonants, blends, math combinations

MATERIALS: Posterboard, tagboard, masking tape, felt pens, scissors

CONSTRUCTION:

Step 1: Cut two pieces of posterboard 10" x 15".

Step 2: Cut sixteen tagboard strips 9" x 1".

Step 3: Space eight of the strips evenly on each piece of posterboard and secure with masking tape, covering the bottom ¼" of each strip.

Step 4: Put masking tape on the ends of each strip to attach securely.

Step 5: Write consonant digraphs on the left side of each strip.

Step 6: Use tape to attach the two pieces of posterboard to make a book.

Step 7: Write questions in riddle form on sixteen 4" x 2" tagboard cards (see illustration for examples).

Step 8: Write the answers on the back of the cards.

PLAYING
DIRECTIONS: The student attempts to guess the answer to each riddle, then puts the card in the pocket by the correct consonant digraph.

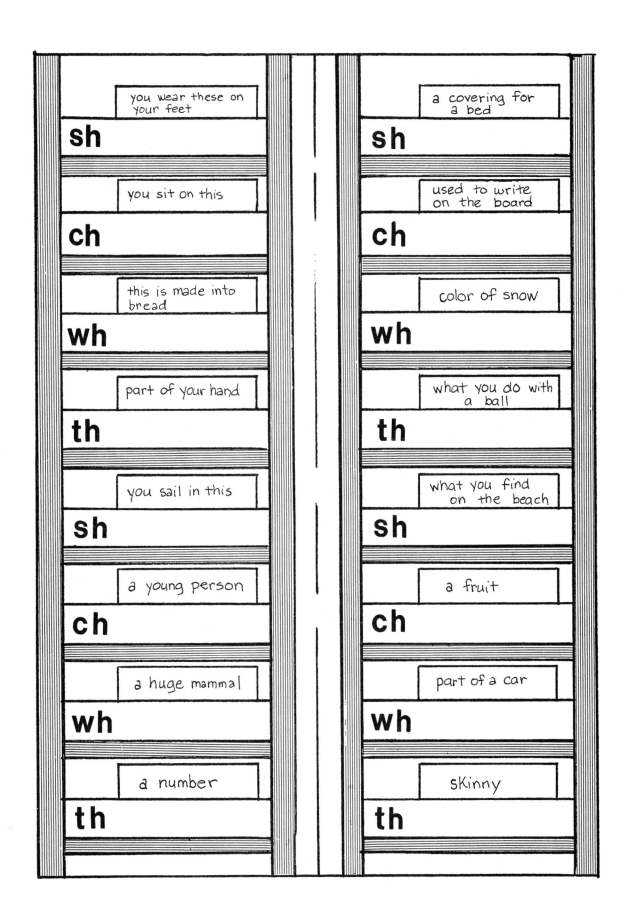

you wear these on your feet	a covering for a bed
sh	**sh**
you sit on this	used to write on the board
ch	**ch**
this is made into bread	color of snow
wh	**wh**
part of your hand	what you do with a ball
th	**th**
you sail in this	what you find on the beach
sh	**sh**
a young person	a fruit
ch	**ch**
a huge mammal	part of a car
wh	**wh**
a number	skinny
th	**th**

CATCH-A-BLEND

SUBJECT AREA: Language Arts

SKILL: Blends

ADAPTABILITY: Math combinations

MATERIALS: Felt pens, construction paper, brad, scissors

CONSTRUCTION:

    Step 1:   Draw and cut out a baseball mitt.

    Step 2:   Make a circle from construction paper for the ball.

    Step 3:   Write a consonant blend on the ball and corresponding endings on the mitt.

    Step 4:   Attach the ball to the mitt with a brad.

PLAYING
DIRECTIONS: The student turns the ball, sounding out each word at every turn. Another student can check to see if the words are being pronounced correctly. If a few mitts are made, they can be used in a group.

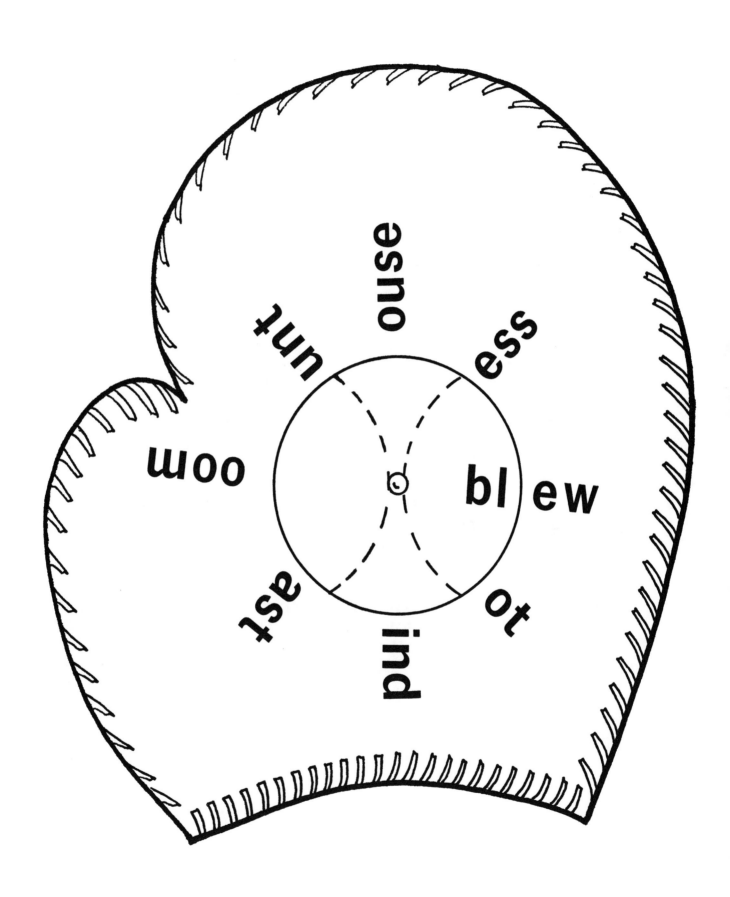

PICK-A-POUCH

SUBJECT AREA:	Language Arts
SKILL:	Long vowels
ADAPTABILITY:	Short vowels, math combinations
MATERIALS:	Brown construction paper, scissors, tagboard, glue, pictures, felt pens, posterboard

CONSTRUCTION:

Step 1: Draw five kangaroos on construction paper.

Step 2: Cut out the kangaroos.

Step 3: Glue a picture on each kangaroo, illustrating a vowel.

Step 4: Staple a pocket to each kangaroo.

Step 5: Cut tagboard cards to fit the kangaroos' pockets.

Step 6: Cut out pictures of words containing long vowels and glue the pictures on the cards.

PLAYING
DIRECTIONS: The student places the picture card in the pocket of the kangaroo with a matching vowel.

I

THE VOWEL VENDER

SUBJECT AREA: Language Arts

SKILL: Short vowels

MATERIALS: Tagboard, felt pens, compass, brads, ruler, scissors, stapler

CONSTRUCTION:

Step 1:   Fold a 9" x 12" piece of tagboard in half to make a 6" x 9" rectangle.

Step 2:   Measuring 3¼" from the left and 2½" from the top, cut three windows, 3¼" square, leaving a tiny strip between each window (see illustration).

Step 3:   Make two 2½" circles.

Step 4:   Divide the circles into eight equal segments.

Step 5:   Write a consonant in each segment.

Step 6:   Attach the wheels onto the back fold of the tagboard with a brad, 1¾" from the edge.

Step 7:   Make a vowel strip 6½" x 3¼".

Step 8:   Write the five vowels on the strip.

Step 9:   Cut slits above and below the middle window and place the vowel strip in slits.

Step 10:   Cut two 1½" x ¾" strips.

Step 11:   Staple the above strips to the top and bottom of the vowel strip to prevent slipping.

PLAYING DIRECTIONS: The student chooses a vowel, turns one wheel while the other remains stationary and sounds out the words, nonsense or not.

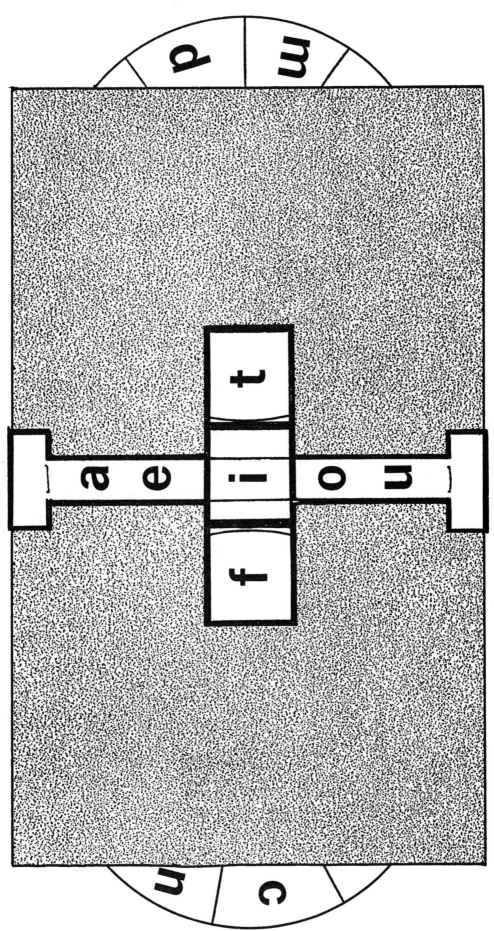

RHYME TIME

SUBJECT AREA: Language Arts

SKILL: Rhyming words

ADAPTABILITY: Math combinations

MATERIALS: Posterboard, tagboard, spinner, felt pens, glue, scissors

CONSTRUCTION:

    Step 1:   Cut posterboard into four identical circles, 4" in diameter.

    Step 2:   Divide each circle into sixteen segments.

    Step 3:   On one of the circles, write words in eight of the segments. Across from each of those words, write rhyming words. This will be the "Rhyming Wheel."

    Step 4:   Cut the other circles into segments.

    Step 5:   On each of the segments, write words that rhyme with those on the Rhyming Wheel.

**PLAYING
DIRECTIONS:**   Two can play. Place word segments face down. One student spins, then draws a segment. If the segment rhymes with the word that the spinner points to, the player gets to keep that segment. If not, the segment goes back to the bottom of the pile. The player with the most segments wins.

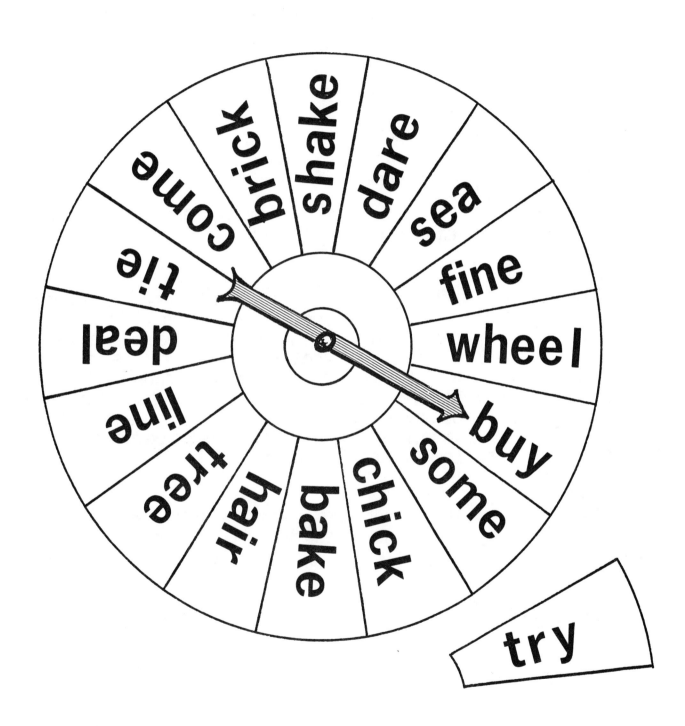

try

QUILT MATCH

SUBJECT AREA: Reading Readiness

SKILL: Visual perception

ADAPTABILITY: Matching activities

MATERIALS: Construction paper or wallpaper samples, posterboard, felt pens, ruler, scissors, glue

CONSTRUCTION:

    Step 1:   Reproduce the two pages of quilt designs. If you prefer, you may make your own designs from construction paper or from wallpaper samples. Glue one sheet of designs on posterboard. Cut the other sheet into cards. At first glance, the two sheets look entirely different; however, the symmetry is identical. For self-checking purposes, number the back of the cards and write the same numerals of the corresponding designs on the back of the posterboard.

PLAYING
DIRECTIONS: The student takes the cards and matches them to the corresponding designs on the posterboard.

SHELVING THE BOOKS

SUBJECT AREA: Language Arts

SKILL: Alphabetizing

ADAPTABILITY: Sequencing activity

MATERIALS: Tagboard, felt pens, X-acto knife, ruler, rubber cement

CONSTRUCTION:

    Step 1:   Reproduce the illustration of books and glue it on tagboard.

    Step 2:   Cut slits along the broken lines at the top and bottom of the books.

    Step 3:   Reproduce the list of book titles and glue it onto tagboard.

    Step 4:   On the back of each title strip, write the number exactly as shown in the illustration at the bottom.

    Step 5:   Cut on the lines, separating the titles.

PLAYING
DIRECTIONS: The student places the book titles in the slits in alphabetical order. The board can be turned over and if the books have been placed correctly, the numbers will appear in sequence.

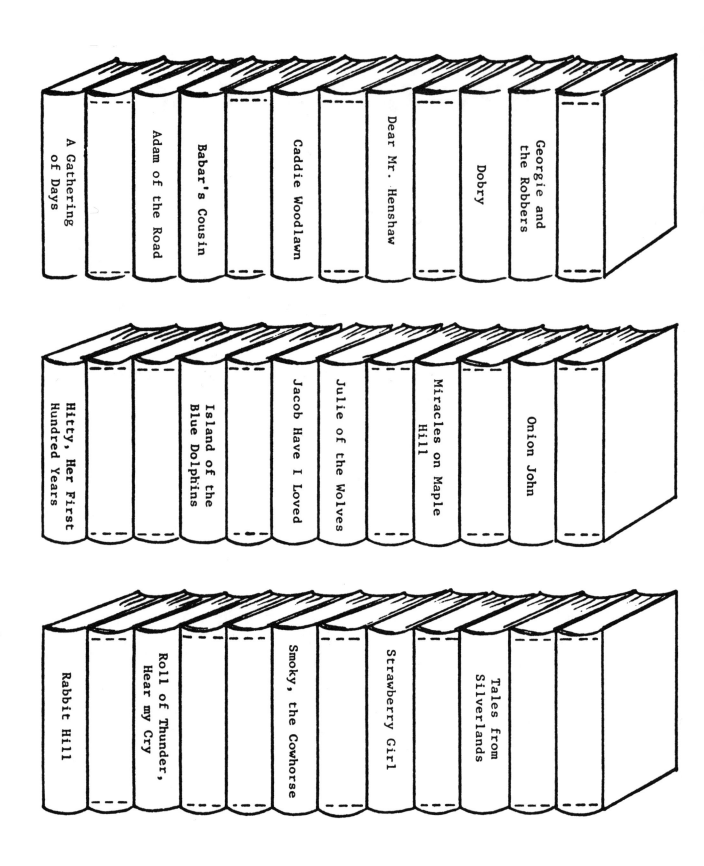

A Gathering of Days

Adam of the Road

Babar's Cousin

Caddie Woodlawn

Dear Mr. Henshaw

Dobry

Georgie and the Robbers

Hitty, Her First Hundred Years

Island of the Blue Dolphins

Jacob Have I Loved

Julie of the Wolves

Miracles on Maple Hill

Onion John

Rabbit Hill

Roll of Thunder, Hear my Cry

Smoky, the Cowhorse

Strawberry Girl

Tales from Silverlands

A Visit to William Blake's Inn	Bridge to Terabithia	Carry on, Mr. Bowditch	Dicey's Song	Ginger Pye
5	4	3	2	1

I, Juan de Pareja	Invincible Louisa	It's Like This, Cat	King of the Wind	Miss Hickory	Puss in Boots
11	10	9	8	7	6

Rifles for Watie	Roller Skates	Shen of the Sea	Sounder	Summer of the Swans	The Grey King	The Westing Game
18	17	16	15	14	13	12

STARDUST

SUBJECT AREA: Reading Readiness

SKILL: Visual discrimination

ADAPTABILITY: Counting, geometric shapes, color recognition

MATERIALS: Posterboard, stick-on stars in several colors, felt pens, straightedge, compass

CONSTRUCTION:

Step 1:   Draw a large, overlapping circle, square, and triangle on the posterboard.

Step 2:   Reproduce twenty copies of the board.

Step 3:   Stick the different colored stars on the board randomly.

Step 4:   Shade in one or more areas on each reproduced sheet and stick one colored star in the corner. No two sheets should be exactly alike.

Step 5:   Write the answers on the back of the sheet in yellow or another light color.

PLAYING
DIRECTIONS: The student will count the number of stars of a particular color in the shaded area on the sheet and then check to see if the answer is correct.

Star-Dust

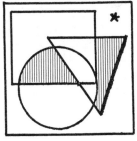

NAME MY COLOR

SUBJECT AREA: Reading Readiness

SKILL: Color and name recognition

ADAPTABILITY: Reading vocabulary

MATERIALS: Colored construction paper, letter stencils, scissors

CONSTRUCTION:

    Step 1:   Trace the letter of each student's name on construction paper, making each letter a different color.

    Step 2:   Cut out the letters.

    Step 3:   Cut each letter into three or four puzzle pieces.

PLAYING
DIRECTIONS: The student matches the pieces of the same color to form a letter, and then arranges the letters to form a name.

ANTONYMS
ALL AROUND

ANTONYMS are opposites. There are five pairs of antonyms spelled out in this puzzle. See if you can find them. Start from the "B" in the first square and move from square to square. You can move in any direction, up, down, side to side, diagonally, but you may use each square only once.

B	L	L	R	Y	O	N	R
A	C	I	G	B	G	O	W
K	W	H	E	A	N	I	T
S	T	I	C	L	R	G	H
T	E	T	N	Y	T	R	I
A	R	F	I	I	S	H	D

_____

_____

_____

_____

_____

CIRCULAR SEARCH

Each of these letter circles represents a word that can be spelled out by starting at the appropriate letter and moving clockwise around the circle. You may use letters over again, but you may not skip a letter. The first one is ORATOR. Good luck with the rest!

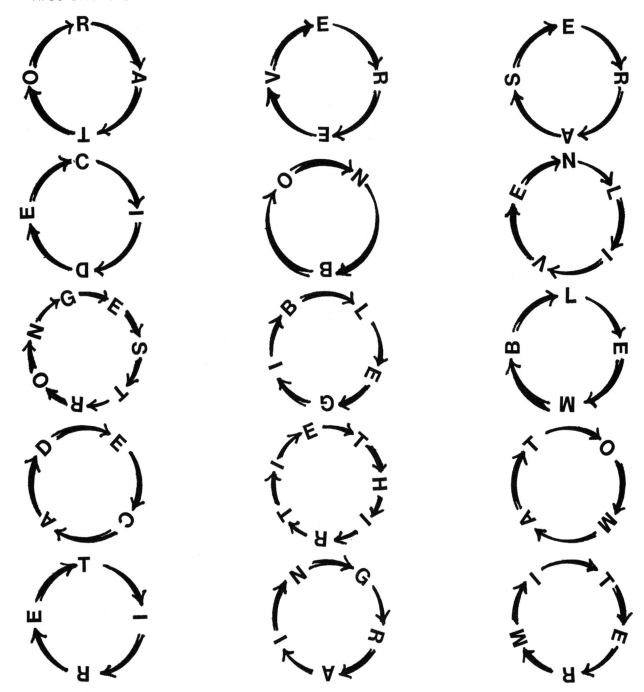

HIDDEN HOMOGRAPHS

A **HOMOGRAPH** is a word identical with another in spelling but differing from it in meaning and sometimes in pronunciation. Fifteen homographs are defined below. Can you match each with its partner and deduce the homograph they define? For example, #1 and f = commune.

1.	converse	a.	grand
2.	month	b.	to bring under control
3.	movement of air	c.	kind of fish
4.	hinged box with mirror	d.	unattractive
5.	topic	e.	opposite
6.	low voice	f.	community
7.	guide	g.	money
8.	understandable	h.	send onward
9.	time	i.	to coil
10.	soft	j.	behavior
11.	race	k.	tiny
12.	to speak to	l.	pressed together
13.	toss	m.	tar
14.	a formal speech	n.	to combine
15.	a large fenced-in area	o.	directions for delivery on letter

_____

_____

_____

_____

_____

_____

WORD WIZARD

Find new words by juggling the letters of the word in bold print.

1. Find a lady in **made**.
2. Find a flower container in **save**.
3. Find part of a shoe in **lose**.
4. Find a body part in **earth**.
5. Find an animal in **shore**.
6. Find some water in **master**.
7. Find a line in **ripest**.
8. Find a ledge in **flesh**.
9. Find announce in **cleared**.
10. Find a friend in **lap**.
11. Find a relaxer in **sap**.
12. Find a sandwich in **bus**.
13. Find a smell in **door**.
14. Find some food in **west**.
15. Find an annoyance in **step**.
16. Find a flower in **sore**.
17. Find a fruit in **lemon**.
18. Find toys in **spot**.

BEAR FACTS

The first letter of each word is missing. Can you fill it in for us?

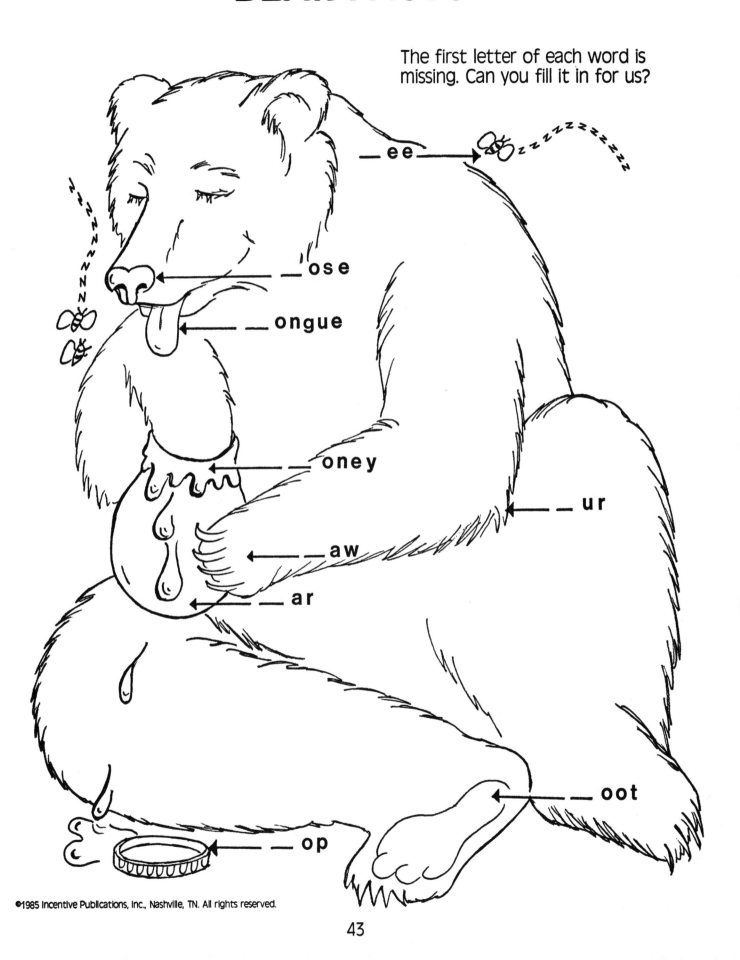

_ee

_ose

_ongue

_oney

_ur

_aw

_ar

_oot

_op

PENTOMINOES

SUBJECT AREA: Math

SKILL: Spatial relationships

MATERIALS: Posterboard, scissors, felt pens, ruler, construction
                  paper, glue

CONSTRUCTION:
   Step 1:   Trace the shapes on posterboard and cut out as shown
                  (illustration A).
   Step 2:   Trace and cut out a second set of shapes from a
                  different color of posterboard (illustration B).
   Step 3:   Trace or draw the grid on construction paper and glue
                  on posterboard.

PLAYING
DIRECTIONS: Each player has a complete set of shapes. The first
                  player places a shape on the grid. The second player also
                  places a shape on the grid. This continues until one
                  player cannot fit any of the remaining shapes on the
                  grid. The last player who can play a piece is the winner.

A

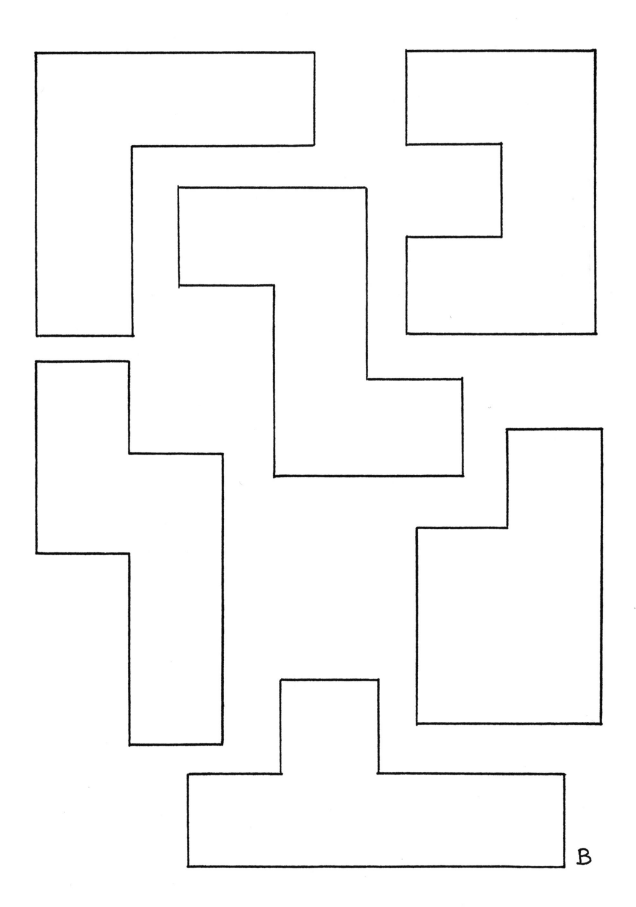

B

47

SAM THE SUM SNAKE

SUBJECT AREA: Math

SKILL: Addition

ADAPTABILITY: Word recognition, subtraction

MATERIALS: Posterboard, felt pens, construction paper, glue

CONSTRUCTION:
  Step 1:   Cut a worm from light-colored construction paper.
  Step 2:   Glue the worm onto posterboard of a contrasting color.
  Step 3:   Decide on number combinations to be used.
  Step 4:   Write a numeral in each segment of the worm (see illustration). Plus and minus signs may be added between the numerals to make the game more challenging.

PLAYING
DIRECTIONS: The student adds the numerals to find as many combinations as possible that add up to a given sum. A numeral may be used more than once, but the order of the numerals may not be changed. For example, $7 + 8 = 15$ and $2 + 5 + 4 + 3 + 1 = 15$ and $2 + 5 + 7 + 1 = 15$ and $2 + 9 + 3 + 1 = 15$ and $3 + 4 + 6 + 2 = 15$.

Sam the sum snake

How many number combinations can you find on Sam that add up to 15? You may use a numeral more than once, but you may not change the order of the numerals.

HOOKED ON NUMBERS

SUBJECT AREA: Math

SKILL: Number sequence

ADAPTABILITY: Color discrimination, comparison of adjectives, alphabetizing

MATERIALS: Large piece of heavy cardboard or plywood, hooks or brads, tagboard, drill, hole punch, felt pens

CONSTRUCTION:

Step 1:   Cut thirty 2" x 3½" tagboard cards.

Step 2:   Write four or five digit numerals on the cards, using the same numerals in a different order. For example, 97,810; 97,081; 95,871; 95,421; 95,214.

Step 3:   Drill holes in the cardboard or plywood, spacing the holes far enough apart to fit the cards.

Step 4:   Insert the hooks in the holes. If brads are used, insert one part of the brad through the cardboard and bend it to make a hook.

PLAYING
DIRECTIONS: The student puts the cards on the hooks in numerical sequence.

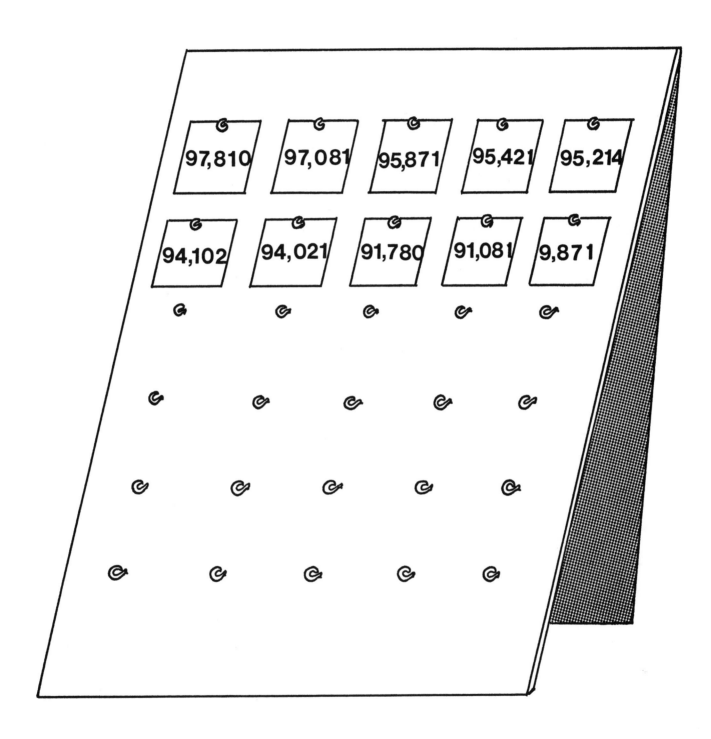

PLACE VALUE BEADS

SUBJECT AREA: Math

SKILL: Place value recognition

MATERIALS: Tagboard, felt pens, beads (preferably in six different colors), heavy twine, hole punch, scissors

CONSTRUCTION:

Step 1:   Cut tagboard into 4½" x 5½" cards.

Step 2:   About ¼" from the bottom edge, punch six holes, the first ⅜" from the edge and at ¾" intervals after that.

Step 3:   On the front of the card, above the first hole on the left, write 100,000; above the next hole, write 10,000; then 1,000, 100, then 10 and finally 1.

Step 4:   Tie a piece of heavy twine through each hole, leaving about 6" hanging.

Step 5:   Write a six-digit number in the middle of the card.

Step 6:   On the back of the card, draw circles to represent beads for each place value, reversing the numbers so that the same string represents the same number on the back as the one on the front (see illustration).

PLAYING
DIRECTIONS: The student uses the beads to illustrate place value by stringing the appropriate number of beads under each value. Cards can be turned over for checking.

517,068

100,000	10,000	1,000	100	10	1

THE KNOW-IT-ALL

SUBJECT AREA: Math

SKILL: Multiplication facts

ADAPTABILITY: Any kind of drill involving question and answer, such as parts of speech, vocabulary, syllabication, leaf identification

MATERIALS: Half-gallon milk carton, X-acto knife, contact paper, posterboard, tape, felt pens, stapler, tagboard

CONSTRUCTION:

Step 1:   Open the top of the carton completely and cover with contact paper.

Step 2:   Make a ¼" wide slit 1¾" from the top where the carton bends (see illustration).

Step 3:   Make a similar slit 1¾" from the bottom of the carton.

Step 4:   Cut a piece of posterboard 13½" x 3¼" and cover with contact paper.

Step 5:   Put the piece of posterboard through the open top of the carton and out the bottom slit.

Step 6:   Staple the piece of posterboard to the front of the carton, even with the top.

Step 7:   Staple the top of the carton shut.

Step 8:   Pull the piece that is sticking out of the bottom slit under the bottom of the carton and tape securely.

Step 9:   Cover the top where the staples are and the bottom where the tape is with additional contact paper.

Step 10:   Cut tagboard cards to fit slits.

Step 11:   Write multiplication problems on the front of each card and put a red dot in the upper right-hand corner.

Step 12:   Write the answers on the back of each card, upside down to the lettering on the front.

PLAYING DIRECTIONS: The student reads and tries to answer the problem on the front of the card. Then, the student inserts the card in the computer, red dot first, and checks the answer when the card comes out of the computer.

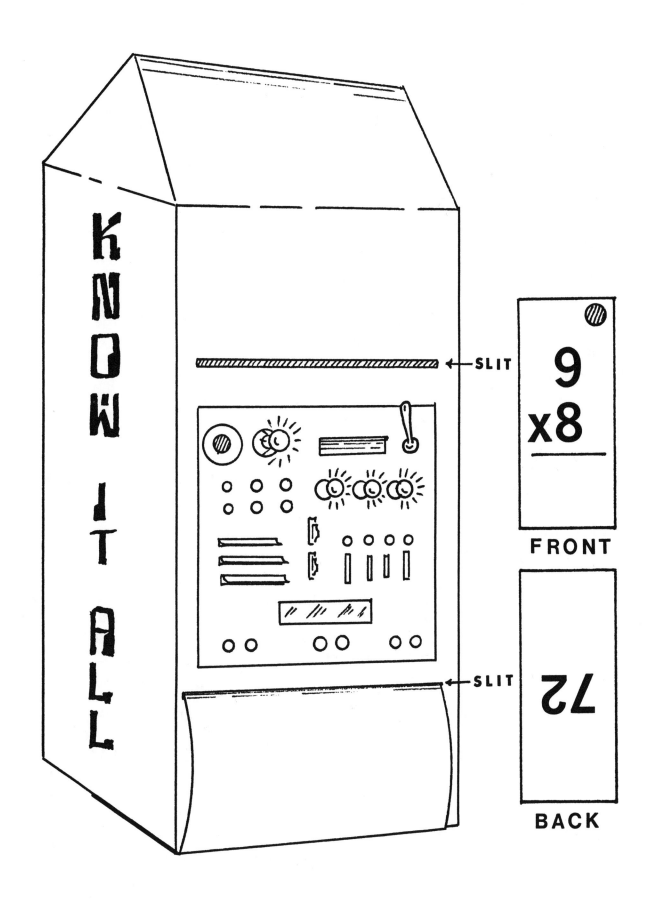

KNOW IT ALL

←SLIT

←SLIT

$$\begin{array}{r} 9 \\ \times 8 \\ \hline \end{array}$$

FRONT

72

BACK

THE NUMBERS GAME

SUBJECT AREA: Math

SKILL: Math operations

ADAPTABILITY: Math facts

MATERIALS: Posterboard, felt pens, glue, scissors, construction paper, three dice, cardboard

CONSTRUCTION:

Step 1: Copy the numbers on construction paper exactly as shown in illustration.

Step 2: Glue the number grid onto posterboard.

Step 3: Cut out sixty-four squares from cardboard the same size as the squares on the grid.

PLAYING DIRECTIONS: The players take turns rolling one die. The player rolling the highest number goes first. The first player rolls all three dice. Using any operations ($+ - \times \div$), the player makes an equation using the three numbers rolled. The player covers the answer to the equation on the board with a square marker. The second player rolls all three dice. This player tries to make an equation with an answer that is next to the covered square. All numbers rolled must be used. Cover the answer. One point is awarded for every covered square adjacent to that answer. The player must play if it is possible to do so. If the player cannot figure out an equation with an answer that is uncovered on the board, the opponent may do so. The opponent then gets the points (if any) and proceeds with a regular turn. At the end of the playing time, the player with the highest score wins.

1	2	3	4	5	6	7	8
9	10	11	12	13	14	15	16
17	18	19	20	21	22	23	24
25	26	27	28	29	30	31	32
33	34	35	36	37	38	39	40
41	42	44	45	48	50	54	55
60	64	66	72	75	80	90	96
100	108	120	125	144	150	180	216

PUZZLING NUMBERS

SUBJECT AREA: Math

SKILL: Math combinations

ADAPTABILITY: Parts of speech, phonics

MATERIALS: A picture, scissors, felt pens, posterboard, rubber cement

CONSTRUCTION:

Step 1:   Cut two pieces of posterboard the size and shape of the picture.

Step 2:   Glue the picture on one piece of posterboard.

Step 3:   Cut the picture into puzzle pieces, all the same basic shape. Be sure to keep the "puzzle" together, so you don't get the pieces mixed up.

Step 4:   Trace the outline of each piece on the other piece of posterboard.

Step 5:   Write a math problem on the back of each puzzle piece and the answer on the corresponding outlined shape on the posterboard.

PLAYING
DIRECTIONS: The student puts the puzzle together by solving the problems.

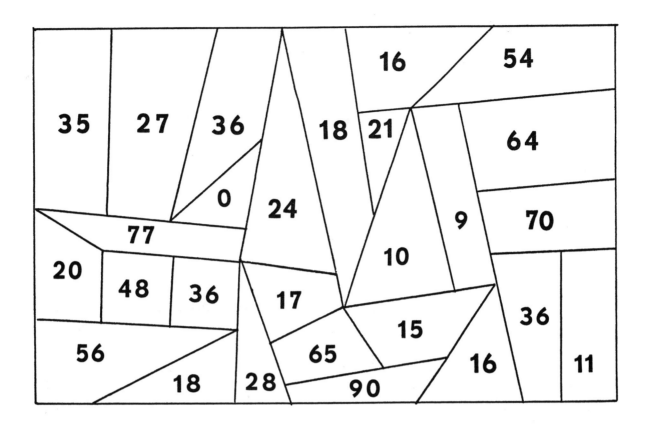

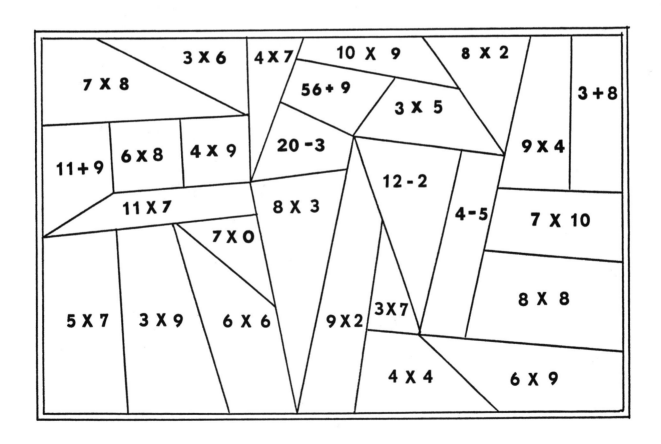

COUNT DOWN

SUBJECT AREA: Math

SKILL: Multiplication and division facts

ADAPTABILITY: Synonyms, Roman numerals, fractions

MATERIALS: Posterboard, tagboard, construction paper, felt pens, magnetic strip, scissors, glue

CONSTRUCTION:

Step 1:   Draw and cut out clouds of light construction paper and glue them on large piece of posterboard.

Step 2:   Draw and cut out rockets of tagboard and cut each into three "stages."

Step 3:   Write math problems on the clouds and two pieces of each rocket. Write the answer on the smallest piece of each rocket.

Step 4:   Glue pieces of magnetic strip on the board above the clouds and on the back of each rocket piece.

PLAYING
DIRECTIONS: The student "builds" rockets by matching the math facts and answers.

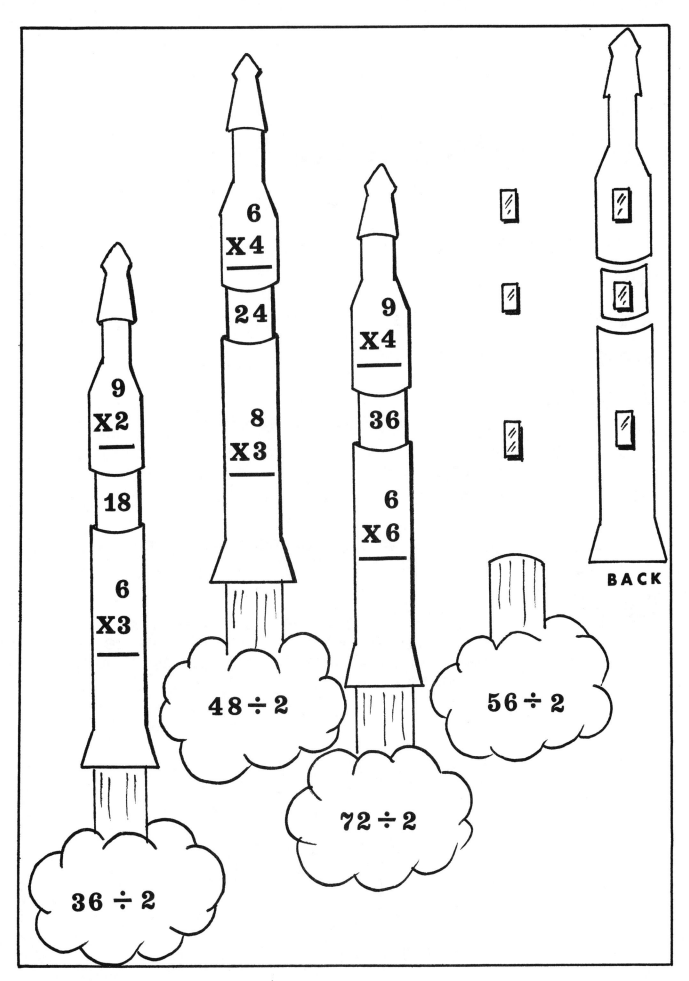

HOLE NUMBERS

SUBJECT AREA: Math

SKILL: Multiplication

ADAPTABILITY: Subtraction, addition, division, phonics

MATERIALS: Tagboard, hole punch, felt pens, scissors

CONSTRUCTION:

Step 1:   Draw numeral shapes on tagboard.

Step 2:   Punch holes about 1" from the edge and about 2" apart from each other.

Step 3:   Write a problem alongside each hole on the front of each card.

Step 4:   Write the answers to the problems alongside the corresponding hole on the back of the card.

PLAYING DIRECTIONS:

Two students can play. One student takes a pencil, pokes it through any hole and gives the answer to the problem alongside that hole. The student on the other side can check the answers.

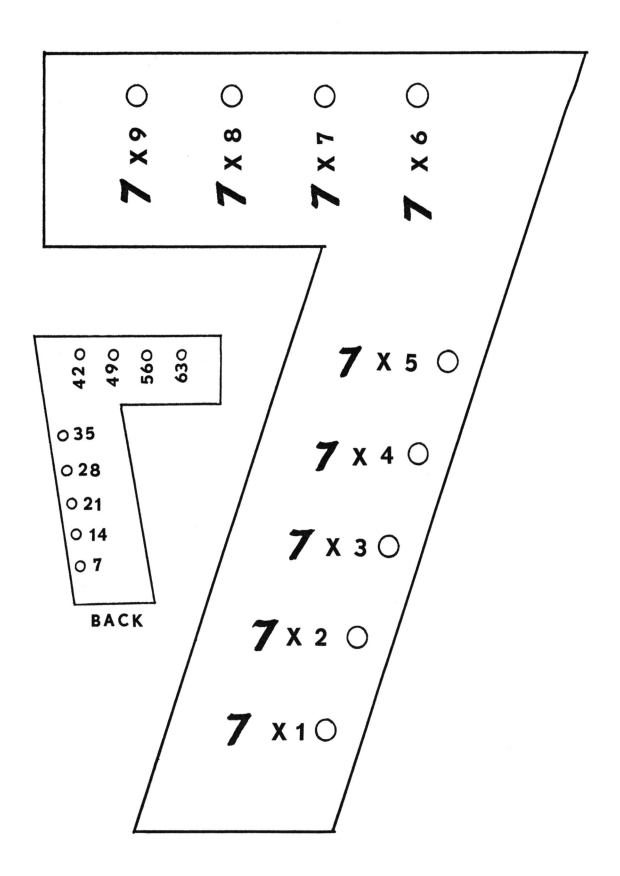

7 x 9 ○
7 x 8 ○
7 x 7 ○
7 x 6 ○

7 x 5 ○
7 x 4 ○
7 x 3 ○
7 x 2 ○
7 x 1 ○

42 ○
49 ○
56 ○
63 ○

○ 35
○ 28
○ 21
○ 14
○ 7

BACK

KLIP THE KLOCK

SUBJECT AREA: Math

SKILL: Multiplication

ADAPTABILITY: Phonics, math combinations

MATERIALS: Posterboard, felt pens, clip-on clothespins, scissors

CONSTRUCTION:

   Step 1:   Cut the posterboard approximately 7½" x 10".

   Step 2:   Divide it into as many parts as desired.

   Step 3:   Write multiplication problems on the front of the board and write matching answers on the back.

   Step 4:   Write the answers to the problems on the clothespins: the numeral answer on one side of the clothespin, and the number word answer on the other.

PLAYING DIRECTIONS: The student clips the clothespin to the posterboard with the correct answer to the problem (number word facing up). After all the problems have been answered, the board is turned over. The answers on the clothespins should be the same as those on the back of the board.

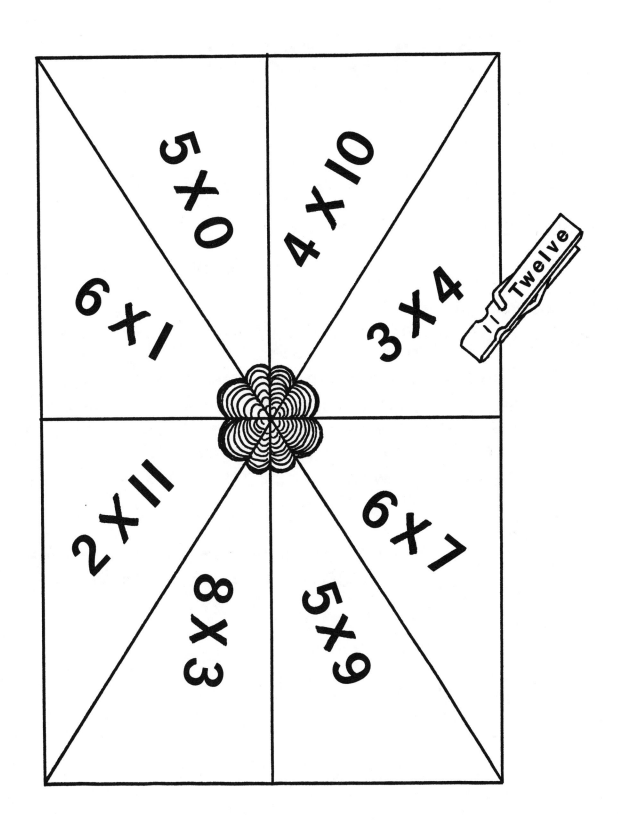

ANIMAL MATCH-UP

SUBJECT AREA: Math

SKILL: Recognition of number words and numerals

ADAPTABILITY: Homonyms, synonyms

MATERIALS: Tagboard or construction paper, felt pens, scissors

CONSTRUCTION:

    Step 1:   Trace or draw simple animals on tagboard or construction paper.

    Step 2:   Cut each animal into three parts.

    Step 3:   Write a numeral on one piece of each animal.

    Step 4:   Write the number word to match the numeral on the second piece of each animal.

    Step 5:   Draw dots illustrating the number on the third piece of each animal.

PLAYING
DIRECTIONS: The student matches the number word, numeral and set. If correctly matched, an animal is formed.

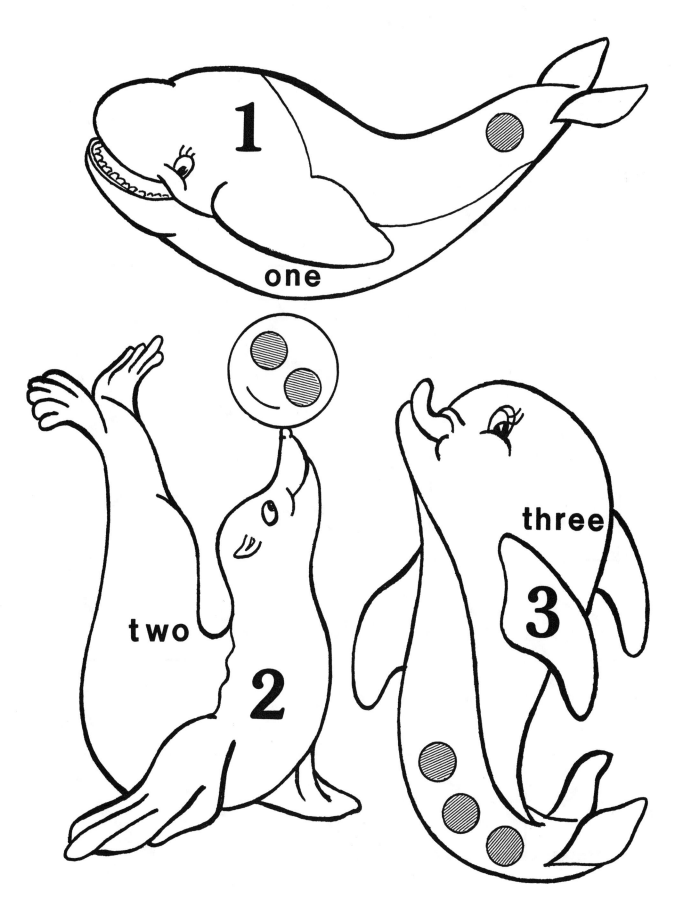

1
one

two
2

three
3

LUCKY 13

How many combinations that equal 13 can you find? Start at the left and go all the way across the row to find the answer to each row. Start at the top and go all the way down the column to find the answer to each column.

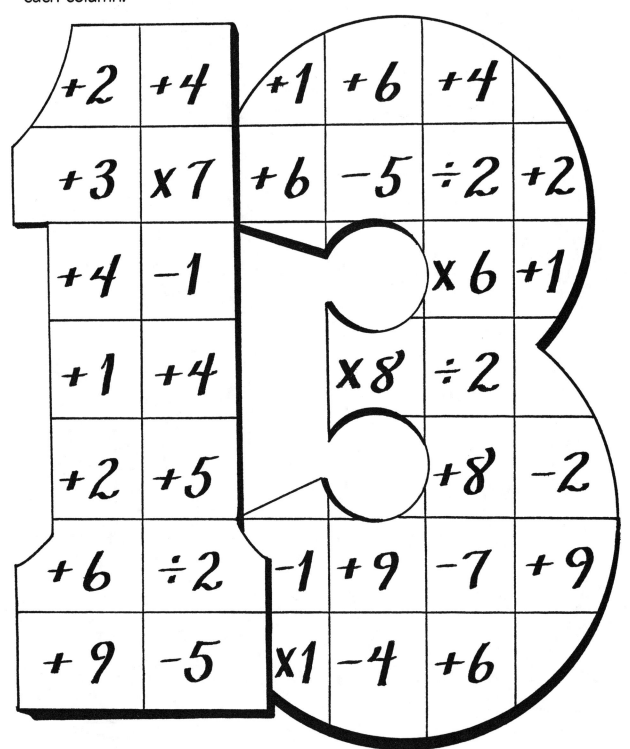

GOING IN CIRCLES

1. Begin by filling in any digit (1 through 9) in outer corner circles.

2. Subtract the smaller number from the larger one and put the answer in the circle between them. Continue subtracting connected circles until you reach the center.

3. Try to get the same number in all four center circles.

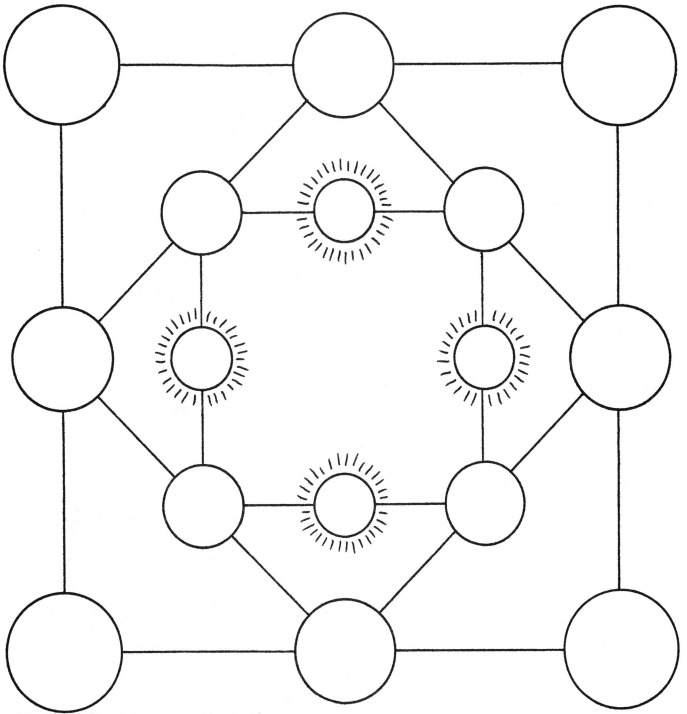

MONEY MATCH

Can you match the famous American with the coin or bill on which his picture appears? (World Book Encyclopedia might be a good source.)

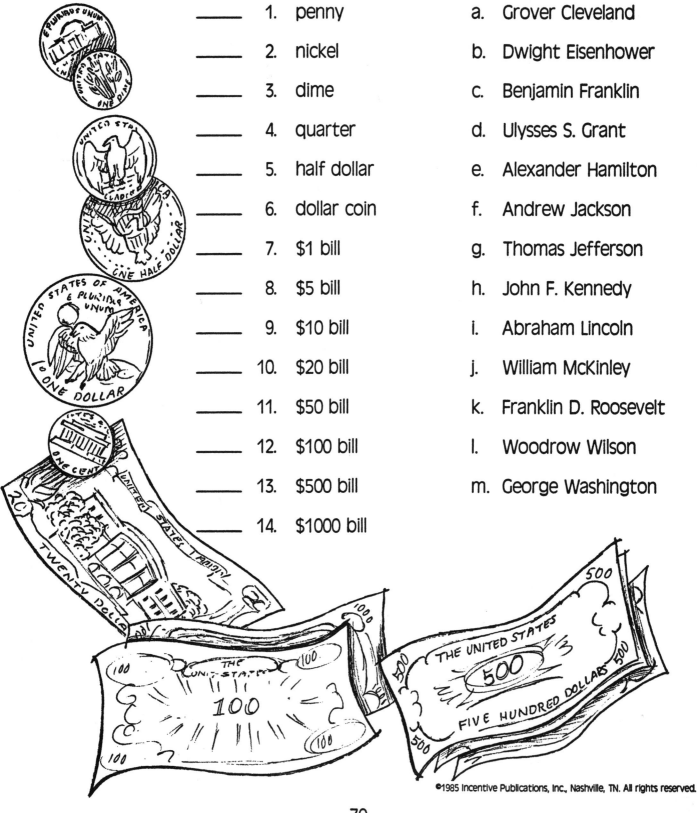

_____ 1. penny

_____ 2. nickel

_____ 3. dime

_____ 4. quarter

_____ 5. half dollar

_____ 6. dollar coin

_____ 7. $1 bill

_____ 8. $5 bill

_____ 9. $10 bill

_____ 10. $20 bill

_____ 11. $50 bill

_____ 12. $100 bill

_____ 13. $500 bill

_____ 14. $1000 bill

a. Grover Cleveland

b. Dwight Eisenhower

c. Benjamin Franklin

d. Ulysses S. Grant

e. Alexander Hamilton

f. Andrew Jackson

g. Thomas Jefferson

h. John F. Kennedy

i. Abraham Lincoln

j. William McKinley

k. Franklin D. Roosevelt

l. Woodrow Wilson

m. George Washington

MAKING CHANGE

Use the information from the "MONEY MATCH" sheet to fill in the blanks below.

1. If you had 6 bills with Alexander Hamilton's picture, you could change them for _____ bills with Andrew Jackson's picture.

2. If you had 10 bills with Ben Franklin's picture, you could change them for _____ bills with William McKinley's picture.

3. If you had 1 bill with Grover Cleveland's picture, you could change it for _____ bills with Ulysses Grant's picture.

4. If you had 20 coins with Franklin D. Roosevelt's picture, you could change them for _____ coins with Dwight Eisenhower's picture.

5. If you had 20 coins with George Washington's picture, you could change them for _____ bills with George Washington's picture.

6. If you had 1 bill with Abraham Lincoln's picture, you could change it for _____ coins with Franklin D. Roosevelt's picture.

7. If you had 2 bills with Alexander Hamilton's picture, you could change them for _____ coins with John F. Kennedy's picture.

8. If you had 60 coins with Thomas Jefferson's picture, you could change them for _____ bills with George Washington's picture.

COORDINATE CODE

Using rectangular coordinates, can you decode the message below? Remember, you go across first and then up in reading rectangular coordinates. Example: G would be (4,1).

(7,1)(2,4)(4,8)(8,3)(1,7)(5,6)   (8,5)(1,7)(4,4)(2,4)
(5,6)(6,2)(8,3)(6,4)(2,2)(2,4)(5,6)   (1,7)(5,6)   (8,8)(2,4)(1,3)
(8,5)(2,6)(8,3)(5,6)(2,4)(5,6)   (6,7)(2,6)

(4,5)(2,6)(1,7)(1,5)(1,7)(5,6)   (8,5)(1,7)(4,4)(2,4)
(2,2)(2,6)(7,3)(4,5)(2,4)(6,2)(5,6)   (1,7)(3,6)(6,7)
(4,8)(2,4)(1,7)(6,7)(1,1)   (2,4)(1,1)(2,4)(5,6)   (6,2)(2,6)(2,6)

(6,4)   (1,7)(8,1)   (1,7)   (8,5)(2,6)(8,1)(2,6)
(5,6)(1,7)(2,2)(6,4)(2,4)(3,6)   (1,7)(3,6)(6,7)   (5,6)(2,6)
(1,7)(8,3)(2,4)   (1,1)(2,6)(7,6)

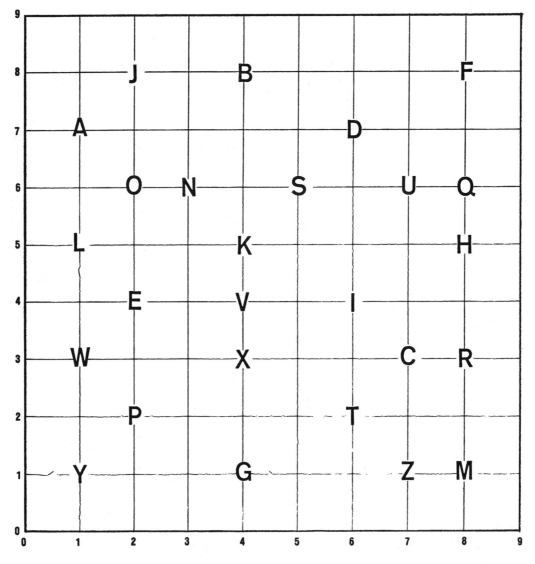

ROAM AROUND ROME

Can you find the Roman landmarks at the following locations using polar coordinates? Example: (290°,7) **Castel Angelo**

1.   (330°,19)_____

2.   (20°,12)_____

3.   (195°,14)_____

4.   (225°,19)_____

5.   (121°,20)_____

6.   (175°,9)_____

7.   (80°,17)_____

8.   (230°,6)_____

9.   (15°,18)_____

10.   (275°,17)_____

11.   (50°,9)_____

12.   (130°,15)_____

13.   (120°,4)_____

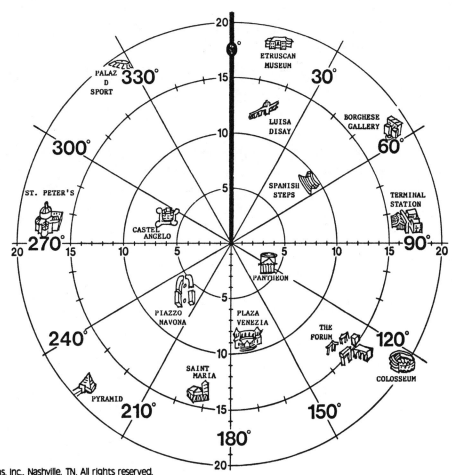

KINGDOM ANIMALIA

SUBJECT AREA: Science

SKILL: Classification of animals

ADAPTABILITY: Rock or leaf classification

MATERIALS: Construction paper, posterboard, glue, felt pens,
                   magnetic strips

CONSTRUCTION:

    Step 1:   Cut tree shape from light brown construction paper
                   and glue on contrasting posterboard.

    Step 2:   Write classification information on each fork of the tree.

    Step 3:   Make construction paper leaves and write animal
                   names on them.

    Step 4:   Glue magnetic strips on branches of the tree and on the
                   backs of the leaves.

PLAYING
DIRECTIONS: The student classifies each animal by placing the leaf on
                   the correct branch of the tree.

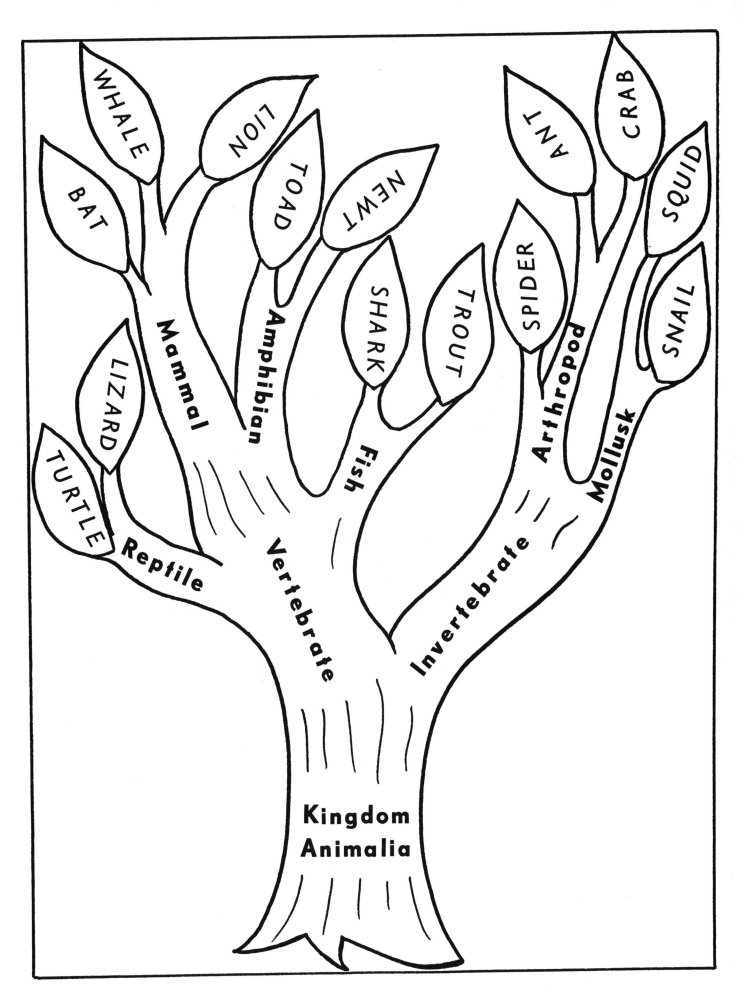

HANG IT RIGHT

SUBJECT AREA: Science

SKILL: Stages of development

ADAPTABILITY: Story sequence

MATERIALS: Manila folder, tagboard, hole punch, paper clips, felt pens, contact paper, science pictures showing stages of development, scissors

CONSTRUCTION:

Step 1:   Cut out science pictures showing development (illustration may be reproduced).

Step 2:   Glue the pictures onto 3" x 4" tagboard cards.

Step 3:   Draw 3½" x 4½" rectangles (to represent frames) on a manila folder.

Step 4:   Punch holes about 1" from the top of each frame.

Step 5:   Twist paper clips to make hooks and poke a paper clip through each hole.

Step 6:   Write numerals under each of the frames to show the order.

Step 7:   Cover the back of the board with contact paper to hide the paper clips.

PLAYING
DIRECTIONS: The student puts the pictures in correct order.

Additional developmental stages that may be used are: egg to chicken; egg to frog; seed to fruit.

CONCENTRATING ON LEAVES

SUBJECT AREA: Science

SKILL: Leaf identification

ADAPTABILITY: Math combinations, phonics, vocabulary, word recognition

MATERIALS: Posterboard, X-acto knife, contact paper, tagboard, felt pens

CONSTRUCTION:

Step 1: Cut two pieces of posterboard 13½" x 17½".

Step 2: Cover one side of each piece of posterboard with contrasting contact paper.

Step 3: On one piece of posterboard, cut twenty 2" x 3½" windows, five across and four down. The windows are ½" from the edge with 1" between them. The rectangles cut from these windows will become cards.

Step 4: Glue the cut-out posterboard frame onto the other piece of posterboard.

Step 5: Trim the posterboard rectangles from the window frame to 2" x 3". You will have twenty cards of two contrasting colors.

Step 6: On one set of cards, draw or glue pictures of various leaves.

Step 7: On the other set of cards, duplicate the pictures or drawings of the leaves and write the names of the leaves under them. These are the answer cards.

PLAYING
DIRECTIONS: Two or more can play. The cards are turned face down on the board. The first player turns up a leaf card and identifies the leaf. The same player then turns an answer card over. If it matches the first card and the leaf has been identified correctly, the player keeps both cards. If the cards do not match or if the leaf has been incorrectly identified, the cards are replaced face down. The player who has the most cards when all the cards have been taken wins.

BEAK, FEET, TREAT

SUBJECT AREA: Science

SKILL: Scientific inferences

ADAPTABILITY: Math facts, homonyms, reading numerals, math symbols

MATERIALS: Posterboard, felt pens, hole punch, aluminum foil, filament tape, cellophane tape, pictures of bird beaks and feet, pictures of bird food (illustration may be reproduced), circuit tester

CONSTRUCTION:

Step 1:   Cut two pieces of posterboard 6" x 9".

Step 2:   Glue pictures of beaks and feet down the right side of one board.

Step 3:   Glue pictures of bird food down the left side of the board. (If board is to be laminated or covered with contact paper, it should be done at this point.)

Step 4:   Punch a hole under each picture at least 1" from the border.

Step 5:   Cut strips of foil about ½" wide and 12" long and fold lengthwise into ¼" x 12" strips.

Step 6:   Turn the board over and tape foil strips connecting the matching holes.

Step 7:   Cover the back of each strip with cellophane tape to hold it firmly in place and to prevent contact with other strips.

Step 8:   Attach remaining piece of the posterboard to the back of the board with filament tape.

PLAYING DIRECTIONS: The student touches the circuit tester ends to the foil spot under each matching illustration. If the match is correct, the light goes on.

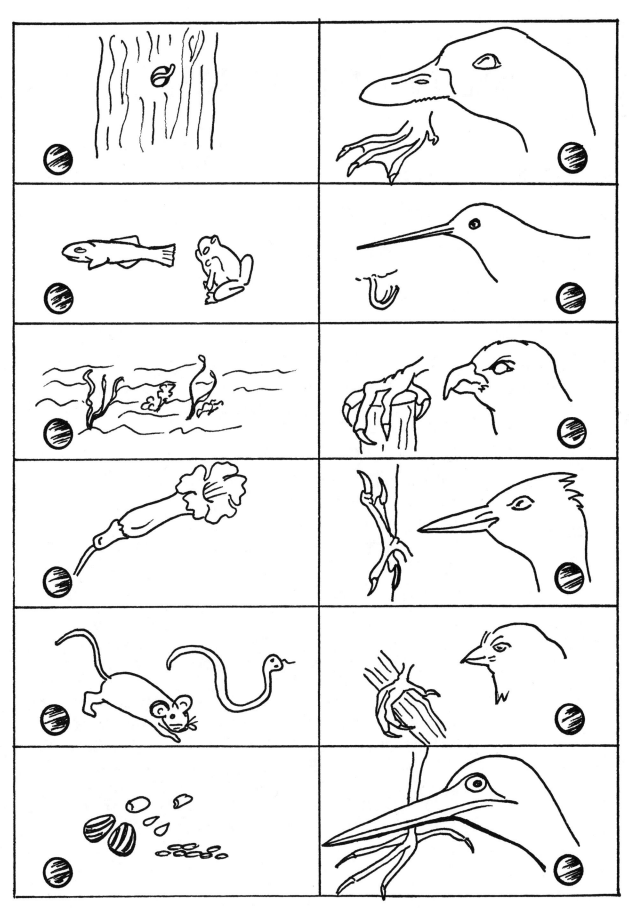

ALL ABOUT ANIMALS

SUBJECT AREA: Science

SKILL: Animal characteristics review

ADAPTABILITY: Classification exercise

MATERIALS: Tagboard, ruler, felt pens, scissors

CONSTRUCTION:

    Step 1:   Cut four tagboard pieces measuring 6½" x 9".

    Step 2:   Draw lines dividing each board into twenty spaces. Sixteen of them should measure 1½" x 2". The remaining four spaces should measure 1" x 1½".

    Step 3:   Cut fifty cards 1½" x 2".

    Step 4:   On the top of each board write the four headings: amphibian, mammal, reptile, bird.

    Step 5:   On the front of each card, write one of the characteristics of the animal, or the name of an animal; and on the back, write the classification (for self-checking purposes).

PLAYING DIRECTIONS: Each player has a board. The cards are placed face up in a stack. The first player takes the top card and places the card under the matching animal classification. To check the answer, turn the card over. If the placement of the card is incorrect, the card should be returned to the bottom of the stack. The next player draws a card from the top of the stack and places it on the board. If the player does not find a vacant space for the card, the card is returned to the stack, and that turn is forfeited. The player who fills up the board first wins.

AMPHIBIAN	MAMMAL	REPTILE	BIRD
eggs usually jelly-like	female provides milk for her young	coldblooded	has feathers
eggs are laid in water	constant body temperature	skin with horny scales	streamlined body
no visible scales	hairy	eggs have a hard or leathery skin	can swim, climb, walk, and perch
usually skin is moist	brain is more complex	lays eggs	migrates in spring and fall

Information for additional cards to **"ALL ABOUT ANIMALS"**

Mammal

Blue whale
Porpoise
Otter
Mole
Bat
Mink
Fisher (weasel)

Bird

Pheasant
Tufted titmouse
Kingfisher
Goldfinch

Reptile

Alligator
Crocodile
Snake
Lizard
Turtle

Amphibian

Lives in the water most of
    the time
Frog
Toad
Salamander
Newt

Shared Characteristics

Constant body temperature (mammal, bird)
Coldblooded (reptile, amphibian)
Lays eggs (bird, reptile, amphibian)
No visible scales (bird, amphibian, mammal)

COLONY CLUES

SUBJECT AREA: Social Studies

SKILL: Revolutionary War history review

ADAPTABILITY: Any series of events involving a certain area

MATERIALS: Posterboard, felt pens, tagboard, glue, construction paper, scissors, eight markers for each student

CONSTRUCTION:

Step 1:   Draw a map of the thirteen colonies on construction paper, marking locations where important events took place.

Step 2:   Cut out the map and glue onto posterboard.

Step 3:   Make 2" x 3" cards out of tagboard (or use 3" x 5" index cards cut in half).

Step 4:   Write important events on the front of the cards. Write the location where the events took place on the back of the cards.

PLAYING
DIRECTIONS: The cards are placed on the board with the event side facing up. The first player takes the top card and tells where the event took place. The card is then turned over and the answer is checked. If the player has given the correct answer, a marker is placed on the location on the map and that card is removed from the stack. If the player has given an incorrect answer, the card is placed at the bottom of the stack and no marker is placed on the board. When all of the events have been correctly located, the game is over and the player with the most markers on the board wins.

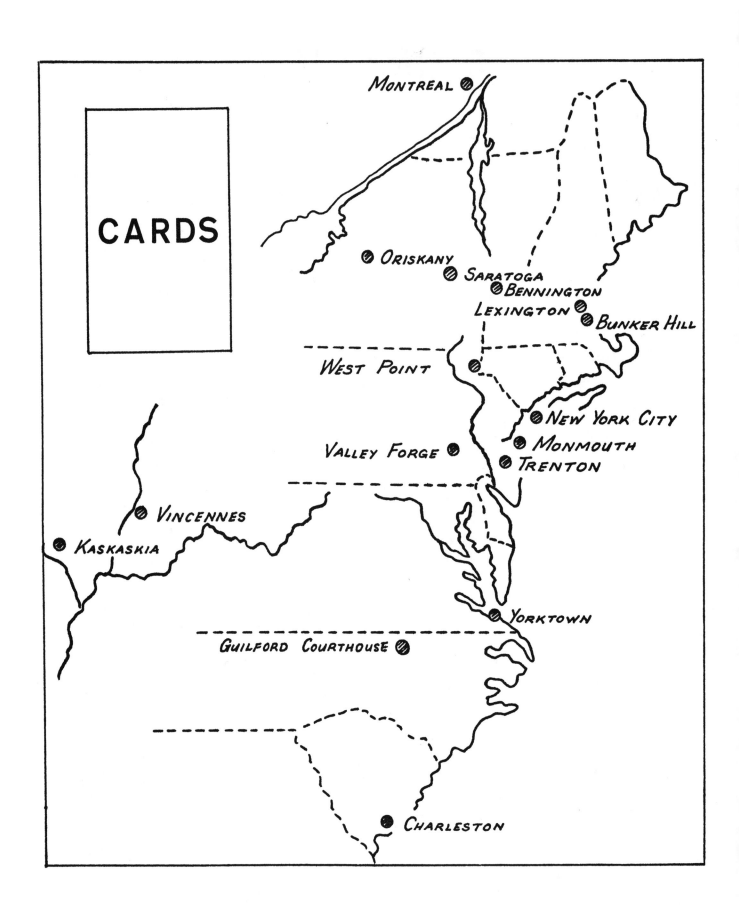

CARDS

MONTREAL

ORISKANY
SARATOGA
BENNINGTON
LEXINGTON
BUNKER HILL

WEST POINT

NEW YORK CITY
MONMOUTH
VALLEY FORGE
TRENTON

VINCENNES

KASKASKIA

YORKTOWN
GUILFORD COURTHOUSE

CHARLESTON

FACTS TO BE USED FOR COLONY CLUES

Lexington:	Paul Revere's famous ride took place here.
Valley Forge:	Washington's army spent the terrible winter of 1777 here.
Oriskany:	Redcoats forced the patriots back here in August, 1777.
Saratoga:	Burgoyne surrendered here in October, 1777.
Bennington:	The patriots crushed the Hessians here in 1777.
Bunker Hill:	The battle during which Colonel William Prescott ordered, "Don't fire until you see the whites of their eyes."
Yorktown:	Cornwallis' forces surrendered here in 1781.
Charleston:	Site of a British victory, May 12, 1780.
Montreal:	Patriots occupied this city in November, 1775.
New York City:	British occupied this city in September, 1776.
Trenton:	Washington mounted a surprise attack here, December 26, 1776.
Kaskaskia:	George Rogers Clark captured this British fort in 1778.
Guilford Courthouse:	Cornwallis clashed with Greene here.
Vincennes:	Clark captured this British fort in February, 1779.
Monmouth:	Last major battle north of Virginia.
West Point:	The fort Benedict Arnold attempted to turn over to the British.

CLAIM A CAPITAL

SUBJECT AREA: Social Studies

SKILL: State and capital identification

ADAPTABILITY: Identification of any geographic area

MATERIALS: Tagboard, felt pens, scissors

CONSTRUCTION:

Step 1: Draw a map of the United States on a piece of tagboard, outlining the states (illustration may be reproduced).

Step 2: Cut the states apart.

Step 3: Write a number on the back of each state.

Step 4: Make answer key on tagboard.

PLAYING DIRECTIONS: The states are placed on the playing surface with the blank side up. The first player chooses a state, names it and tells its capital. The answer is checked by looking at the number on the back and checking the answer key. If the player has given the correct information, the state is "claimed" by the player. If the information given is incorrect, the state is returned to the pile. The second player takes a turn. A state that has just been returned to the pile may not be chosen for the remainder of that round; and a player who has given incorrect information about a state, may never choose that state again. The game is over when all the states have been "claimed." The person with the most states wins.

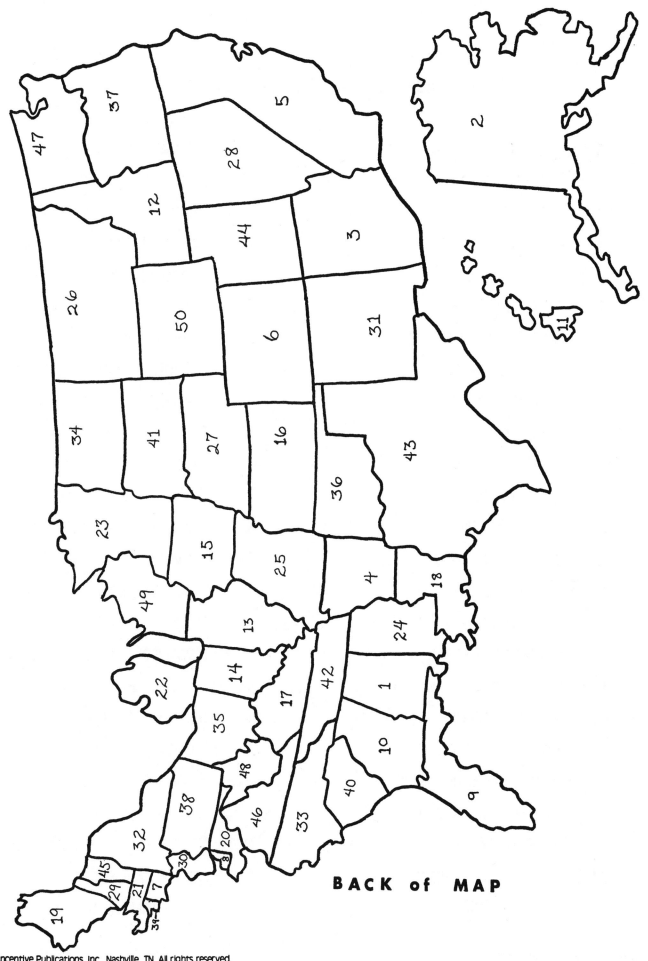

BACK of MAP

ANSWER KEY TO "CLAIM A CAPITAL"

1 — Montgomery, Alabama

2 — Juneau, Alaska

3 — Phoenix, Arizona

4 — Little Rock, Arkansas

5 — Sacramento, California

6 — Denver, Colorado

7 — Hartford, Connecticut

8 — Dover, Delaware

9 — Tallahassee, Florida

10 — Atlanta, Georgia

11 — Honolulu, Hawaii

12 — Boise, Idaho

13 — Springfield, Illinois

14 — Indianapolis, Indiana

15 — Des Moines, Iowa

16 — Topeka, Kansas

17 — Frankfort, Kentucky

18 — Baton Rouge, Louisiana

19 — Augusta, Maine

20 — Annapolis, Maryland

21 — Boston, Massachusetts

22 — Lansing, Michigan

23 — St. Paul, Minnesota

24 — Jackson, Mississippi

25 — Jefferson City, Missouri

26 — Helena, Montana

27 — Lincoln, Nebraska

28 — Carson City, Nevada

29 — Concord, New Hampshire

30 — Trenton, New Jersey

31 — Santa Fe, New Mexico

32 — Albany, New York

33 — Raleigh, North Carolina

34 — Bismarck, North Dakota

35 — Columbus, Ohio

36 — Oklahoma City, Oklahoma

37 — Salem, Oregon

38 — Harrisburg, Pennsylvania

39 — Providence, Rhode Island

40 — Columbia, South Carolina

41 — Pierre, South Dakota

42 — Nashville, Tennessee

43 — Austin, Texas

44 — Salt Lake City, Utah

45 — Montpelier, Vermont

46 — Richmond, Virginia

47 — Olympia, Washington

48 — Charleston, West Virginia

49 — Madison, Wisconsin

50 — Cheyenne, Wyoming

RING IN THE FACTS

SUBJECT AREA: Social Studies

SKILL: Historical figure facts

ADAPTABILITY: Any matching game

MATERIALS: Posterboard, felt pens, scissors

CONSTRUCTION:

    Step 1:   Draw a picture of the Liberty Bell.

    Step 2:   Divide the bell into fourteen sections as shown in the illustration.

    Step 3:   Write the names of the people as illustrated.

    Step 4:   Cut the bell into the fourteen sections.

PLAYING
DIRECTIONS: One student can play. The student puts the bell together by following the printed directions.

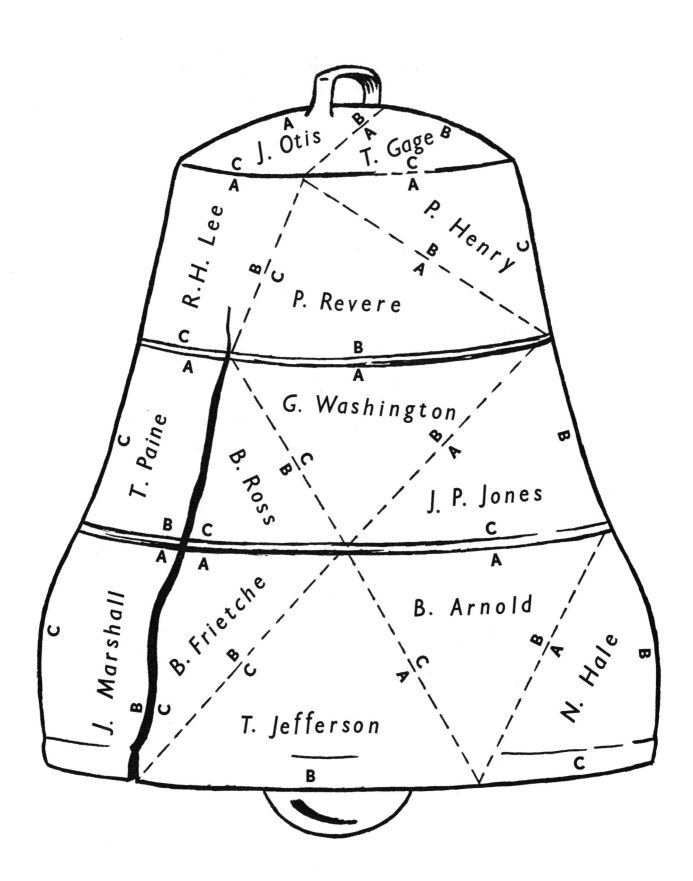

PLAYING DIRECTIONS FOR "RING IN THE FACTS"

1. Place the piece that has the name of the man who proposed the Stamp Act Congress, on the top of your playing area.

2. The piece with the name of the British commander who was made governor of Massachusetts: Place the A side touching the B side of the piece that was just put down.

3. The piece with the name of the man who proposed to Congress that the colonies should be free and independent states: Place the A side touching the C side of the piece in #1.

4. The piece with the name of the author of <u>Common Sense</u>: Place the A side touching the C side of the piece in #3.

5. The piece with the name of the person during whose funeral service the Liberty Bell cracked: Place the A side touching the B side of the piece in #4.

6. The piece with the name of the person who said, "Give me liberty or give me death": Place the A side touching the C side of the piece in #2.

7. The piece with the name of the man who warned the minutemen that the British were on their way to attack Lexington and Concord: Place the A side touching the B side of the piece in #6.

8. The piece with the name of the commander in chief of the Continental Army: Place the A side touching the B side of the piece in #7.

9. The piece with the name of the man who captured more than 300 British ships as captain of the Bonhomme Richard: Place the A side touching the B side of the piece in #8.

10. The piece with the name of the man who committed treason: Place the A side touching the C side of the piece in #9.

11. The piece with the name of the man who wrote the Declaration of Independence: Place the A side touching the C side of the piece in #10.

12. The piece with the name of the man who said, "I only regret that I have but one life to lose for my country": Place the A side touching the C side of the piece in #10.

13. The piece with the name of the person who made the American flag: Place the B side touching the C side of the piece in #8.

14. The piece with the name of the person who said, "Shoot if you must this old gray head but spare your country's flag": Place the A side touching the C side of the piece in #13.

ANSWER KEY

ANTONYMS ALL AROUND
page 39

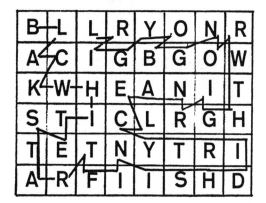

CIRCULAR SEARCH
page 40

orator	emblem
revere	decade
eraser	thirtieth
decide	tomato
bonbon	retire
enliven	ingrain
strongest	termite
legible	

HIDDEN HOMOGRAPHS
page 41

2 - a	August	11 - h	relay
3 - i	wind	12 - e	converse
4 - l	compact	13 - m	pitch
5 - b	subject	14 - o	address
6 - c	bass	15 - n	compound
7 - j	conduct		
8 - d	plain		
9 - k	minute		
10 - 6	tender		

WORD WIZARD
page 42

1.	dame	10.	pal
2.	vase	11.	spa
3.	sole	12.	sub
4.	heart	13.	odor
5.	horse	14.	stew
6.	stream	15.	pest
7.	stripe	16.	rose
8.	shelf	17.	melon
9.	declared	18.	tops

LUCKY 13
page 68

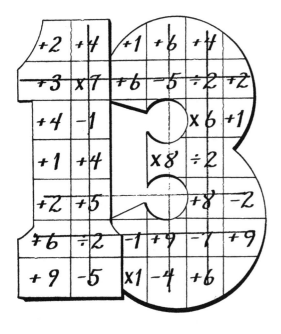

GOING IN CIRCLES
page 69

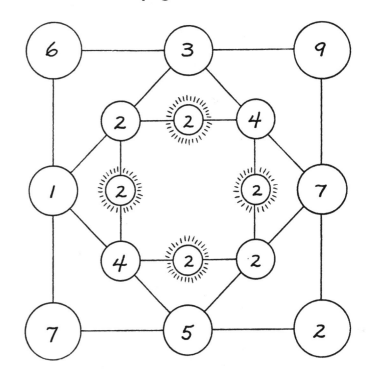

Several solutions are possible.

MONEY MATCH
page 70

1 - i
2 - g
3 - k
4 - m
5 - h
6 - b
7 - m

8 - i
9 - e
10 - f
11 - d
12 - c
13 - j
14 - a

MAKING CHANGE
page 71

1. 3
2. 2
3. 20
4. 2
5. 5
6. 50
7. 40
8. 3

COORDINATE CODE
page 72

Zebras have stripes as few horses do.
Koalas have pockets and beady eyes, too.
I am a homosapien and so are you.

ROAM AROUND ROME
page 73

1. Palaz d Sport
2. Luisa Disay
3. Saint Maria
4. Pyramid
5. Colosseum
6. Plaza Venezia
7. Terminal Station
8. Piazzo Navona
9. Etruscan Museum
10. St. Peter's
11. Spanish Steps
12. The Forum
13. Pantheon